Igor do Nascimento S. de Almeida

Study of Vulnerability to Data Collection by the Phishing Scam Technique

Igor do Nascimento S. de Almeida

Study of Vulnerability to Data Collection by the Phishing Scam Technique

Study carried out at FATEC Botucatu

ScienciaScripts

Imprint
Any brand names and product names mentioned in this book are subject to trademark, brand or patent protection and are trademarks or registered trademarks of their respective holders. The use of brand names, product names, common names, trade names, product descriptions etc. even without a particular marking in this work is in no way to be construed to mean that such names may be regarded as unrestricted in respect of trademark and brand protection legislation and could thus be used by anyone.

Cover image: www.ingimage.com

This book is a translation from the original published under ISBN 978-3-330-99727-1.

Publisher:
Sciencia Scripts
is a trademark of
Dodo Books Indian Ocean Ltd. and OmniScriptum S.R.L publishing group

120 High Road, East Finchley, London, N2 9ED, United Kingdom
Str. Armeneasca 28/1, office 1, Chisinau MD-2012, Republic of Moldova, Europe
Managing Directors: Ieva Konstantinova, Victoria Ursu
info@omniscriptum.com

Printed at: see last page
ISBN: 978-620-8-61292-4

"You're software, not hardware...
Yes... an executable programme with a body." Serial Experiments Lain 11

"Every failure teaches man something he needs to learn."

SUMMARY

CHAPTER 1	4
CHAPTER 2	6
CHAPTER 3	20
CHAPTER 4	31
CHAPTER 5	35
CHAPTER 6	36
CHAPTER 7	39

SUMMARY

Companies invest a lot in technology, but tend to minimise the importance of a very vulnerable factor: the human being. This is the target of social engineering, a technique focused on acting on the **"weakest link in the company".** A widely used tool for these attacks is the **Phishing Scam** technique, which presents attractive promotions and themes, obtaining important information from its targets and thus causing serious damage and problems for companies and individuals. The aim of this work was to analyse the efficiency of this technique at the Botucatu Faculty of Technology (FATEC) by implementing a registration site, identifying the section of the population that is most affected and aiming to improve information security, which is an increasingly valuable asset and a differentiator for companies. Using the **Phishing Scam** technique, database tools such as Navicat and Mysql and Dreamweaver for creating **web** pages, a site was developed and deployed on the Fatec Botucatu web server, where the efficiency of this technique in collecting personal data from users of the pages could be proven, and then misused by malicious people.

Keywords: Social Engineering, Phishing Scam, Information Security

CHAPTER 1

INTRODUCTION

Information is of the utmost importance to an organisation's business and needs to be properly protected. Realising this importance, companies began to worry about keeping this information safe. This gave rise to the term Information Security, which is the protection of information against the most varied types of threat, in order to guarantee business continuity (VICTÓRIA, 2007).

According to Peixoto (2006), information security has become a highlight nowadays, as organisations are looking for practical and effective solutions that can optimise their activities and, at the same time, ensure the security of their working mechanisms. However, as is often the case, organisations focus their attention on technology and underestimate the weakest link that governs all companies in any sector: the human factor. In this context, social engineering has emerged because, in addition to hackers and viruses, dissatisfied employees can pass on improper information.

Marciano and Lima-Marques (2006) state that the increasingly widespread use of computerised systems to carry out the most diverse activities, their integration and the integration of their databases through networks is a determining factor in the information society. However, this information is subject to various forms of threats, both physical and virtual, which seriously jeopardise the security of people and transactions involving the user - system - information complex. This growing situation makes the scenario perfect for **phishing**, where unscrupulous individuals use technology and abuse people's good faith to obtain useful information.

1.1 Objective

The aim of this work was to analyse the vulnerability of the weakest link in organisations, people, to giving up information through Social Engineering, together with the **Phishing** technique, by collecting data through registration links on attractive websites.

1.2 Justifications

Over time, organisations have come to realise the importance of information in their decision-making processes, making it a major differentiating factor. And with this realisation came the need to protect this valuable asset. However, at the same time, there is another side endeavouring to obtain this information at any cost.

However, employees' personal information is also valuable, not just that related to company management, and can lead to serious problems if it gets into the wrong hands.

This study analysed how people at FATEC Botucatu are prepared against these attacks by means of a technique that has been increasingly used to the point of being cited as the crime of the 21st century, the **Phishing** technique (OLLMANN, 2008).

CHAPTER 2

LITERATURE REVIEW

2.1 Social Engineering

Eiras (2004) stated that no matter how powerful and well-configured firewalls, biometrics and all security systems are, they all prove ineffective against a well-crafted social engineering attack.

According to Mitnick and Simon (2003), to break through security barriers, an attacker, an intruder or a social engineer finds a way to trick a trusted user into revealing information or must trick someone important into providing access. When trusted employees are manipulated in favour of the attacker, no technology in the world can protect the company.

Social engineers mix trust, the desire for utility, sympathy and beliefs to get what they want, and they can take on many faces. What makes the work of social engineers much easier is that we are not aware of the threat, particularly in the Western world. Where individuals are taught not to be suspicious of each other. Christian upbringing guides us **to "love our neighbour" and to have trust and faith in each** other. In addition, most people assume that they won't be deceived, believing that this probability is very low; the attacker, understanding this as a common belief, carries out his attack in such a discreet way that he doesn't arouse suspicion while exploiting the victim's trust.

Generally, the invasion of a company's security begins with the intruder obtaining some information or document that seems very innocent, so common and unimportant that most people in the organisation see no reason why it should be protected and restricted. So a company can have the best security technologies on the market, have trained its employees so well that they protect all the secrets at the end of the day and can have hired guards for the building from the best security company there is, and yet that company will still be vulnerable. People can follow the best security practices recommended by experts, they can install every security product and keep a close eye on the progress of the system and the application of security patches. These individuals will still be completely vulnerable. That's because the human factor is the weakest link in security.

Social engineering basically means looking for vital information about a particular person, company, product or organisation. It is the term used for obtaining important information about an organisation through its employees and collaborators. This information can be obtained through naivety or trust. These attacks can be carried out via phone calls, e-mail, chat rooms and even in person (UBRICH; DELLA VALLE, 2006).

2.1.1 The Profile of the Social Engineer

For Eiras (2004), the **hacker** can be considered a type of social engineer. Not every social engineer is a hacker, but in some cases the hacker is a social engineer, with behaviour similar to capturing information. The hacker acts in such a way as to exploit technical vulnerabilities much more, while the social engineer exploits human vulnerabilities.

The social engineer works like no other on points relating to human psychology, exploiting feelings such as fear and insecurity on the part of the victim. They also use sympathy or even guilt.

Successful social engineers are charming, polite and easy to please, social traits necessary to establish rapport and trust. These categories give experienced social engineers a good ability to deal with people, gaining access to virtually any target information using the strategies and tactics of their skill (MITNICK; SIMON, 2003).

2.1.2 Types of Attack

Attacks by social engineers fall into two categories:

Indirect attack: practised by using hacking tools (such as trojans and websites with malicious code) and imposture (such as fake letters, emails and websites that look real) to obtain personal information.

Direct attack: These are characterised by personal contact. They are usually carried out by fax, telephone or even in person. They require a great deal of advance planning, several emergency plans for each of the attack phases and a little artistic flair. A good attacker must be well-articulated so that their plan is not unmasked and also have quick thinking to find ways out if it goes wrong (UBRICH; DELLA VALLE, 2006).

2.1.3 The Tools of the Social Engineer

According to Eiras (2006), the tools of the social engineer are:

- **Telephone or VoIP (Voice over IP):** Impersonating someone you're not would be one of the typical social engineering attacks and, with the knowledge of some jargon or specific knowledge, this would be even easier over the phone.

According to DAWEL (2005), with the characteristics of a respectful, attentive and polite person, one can easily engage another in a telephone conversation and provide the information that the person on the other end of the line wants.

- **Internet (Information gathering):** Such as sites that provide default usernames and passwords, cloned or **File Transfer Protocol** (FTP) sites, dating sites or search engines, and sites with **phishing** registrations.

- **Intranet (remote access):** Something very likely to happen. For example, through remote access, the microphone of a particular user on the network is captured and used as it pleases.

E ***E-mail:*** *E-mails* with false requests for registrations or updates that are actually Trojan horses or promises that require a small registration to win something (social engineering in conjunction with *phishing scam*).

- ***In Person (In Person Social Engineering):*** This type of attack is rarer. The social engineer, with his great powers of persuasion and ability to converse, adopts a whole staging, manipulating the victim to perfection. This tool becomes more powerful when the attacker already knows the target and has information that helps him persuade the victim, sometimes even using confidential information. Some of the resources in favour of the social engineer are seduction, intimidation, drama and credibility.

- ***Chats*** **(Chat or *Messengers*)***:* It's easy to impersonate someone else through chat channels. What's more, photos can be sent, making the conversation even more attractive and making it easier to seduce the victim into getting the information you want.

- **Fax:** First of all, you need to get the fax number of the organisation so that you can start your attack. It follows practically the same principles as e-mail, sending, for example, requests, filling in forms and waiting for replies.

- **Letters/Correspondence:** It's not a very modern medium, but it's a powerful resource that makes older people the main victims. Not just the elderly, but especially those who have a certain resistance to technology. It's very easy to design letters and documents with logos, giving the impression that they really come from that source.

- ***Spyware:*** **"Spy"** *software* **used to** covertly **monitor** the activities of the target computer and which can be installed on the victim's computer using the other tools.

- ***UDumpsted diving")***: Various things that are discarded into the rubbish often contain information that is essential to the supposed social engineer.

Rubbish is an excellent source of information (SÊMOLA, 2000).

- **Over-the-shoulder surfing:** This is the act of observing a person typing on a computer keyboard in order to discover passwords or other user information. Care should be taken when typing passwords in public places where there is a good flow of people.

- **P2P** ***(Peer-to-Peer):*** Technology where communication is established between numerous computers, like a network. These applications are examples of how social engineering can be carried out, due to some of the features they offer, such as sending messages, **showing IP's or names, in short, the communication itself can already be** a favourable factor for the Social Engineer.

2.1.4 The Techniques of a Social Engineer

Eiras (2006) stated that a social engineer uses the following techniques:

- **Harmless vs. Valuable Information:** Information is broken down into parts, some important and some not, which, when combined with the other parts, will form the final result. Thus, information that appears to be irrelevant or not considered important at all, when put together with other information that is also considered important, takes on a different form to what was thought to be harmless.

- **Creating Trust:** What the social engineer does through good conversation is to gain the trust of the victim and, with his skills, reinforces this bond of friendship created, until he can then attack and get the information.

- **Simply Asking:** Considered literally the simplest technique for getting information. When you have a question or want some information, the natural thing to do is to ask, so nothing is more practical than simply asking the supposed victim for the information you want.

"Never think that social engineering attacks need to have **elaborate *lies* so complex that they will probably be recognised before they are completed.**

Some are direct, quick and very simple attacks, which are nothing more than... well, *(iMplesicmte (MIÍT as (nfoTmaçÕKS.* " (MITNICK; SIMON, 2003)

The social engineer undoubtedly has tricks for obtaining the simplest to the most confidential information within a particular company.

- **Can I help you?:** With their brilliant persuasion skills, the attacker creates a problem and takes advantage of it, circumventing the situation and becoming the exact solution to your problems. This type of attack, known as reverse social engineering, is extremely powerful. With it, the social engineer is able to gain absolute credibility in order to obtain the information they want.

Mitnick and Simon (2003) stated that simple knowledge of internal terminology can make a social engineer appear to assume authority and knowledge. The attacker almost always uses this common misconception to get what they want from their victims.

- **Could you help me?:** One of the most powerful methods used is to pretend to need help. Bearing in mind that the new or old employee of the house, seeing the **simple need to be able to help a "fellow worker" who has just** asked for information, will not hesitate to co-operate and thus provide what they want.

According to Mitnick and Simon (2003), it is human nature to trust our colleagues, particularly when the request passes the test of being reasonable. Social engineers use this knowledge to exploit their victims and achieve their goals.

- **Social Engineering on the Internet:** Traps such as cloned websites, misleading messages that arrive in our e-mail - *fakemail* (fake e-mails) with apparently harmless attachments and chats (chats) are tools often used by the social engineer.

Programmes that are inserted into computers, most often by ourselves, persuaded or induced by someone (social engineer) or for some reason (interesting and attractive adverts via e-mail), are some of the problems that can arise. The user should be aware of *malware* - short for *malicious software* - which, if executed, can even give you full access to your computer, as if the attacker were sitting in front of your machine using your keyboard.

2.2 **The** Phishing **Technique**

For Milletary (2005), the **term** *"hhihhmg"* **originated in the mid-1990s**, when it was used to describe the acquisition of account information from Internet *Service Providers* (ISPs). But today the term covers a variety of attacks targeting personal information.

Originally, *phishing* was identified as the use of *email* messages designed to look like messages from trusted agents, such as banking or sales websites, or as a validation of your account information. These messages usually use a sense of urgency (such as a threat of account suspension) to motivate the user to take action. Recently, new social engineering techniques are emerging to trick unsuspecting users. These include offering to fill in a survey for an *online* bank, receiving a cash reward if users include their account information, *email* messages claiming to be from hotel rewards clubs, asking the user to confirm their credit card information in order to get a booking. Included in these messages is a *link* for the victim's use, which directs the user to a website where they can enter their personal information. This site is modelled on the legitimate site. The information is then collected and used by the criminal. These fake *emails* and websites have constantly evolved to become more imperceptible to casual investigation.

Recently, the definition of *phishing* has expanded to cover a wider variety of electronic financial crimes. In addition to the widespread use of these fake emails and websites to trick users into divulging their personal information, there has been an increase in the amount of malicious code targeting specific user account information. Once installed on the victim's computer, these programmes use various techniques to spy on communications and collect account information. This method differs from the technical subterfuge usually associated with *phishing scams* and can be included without the definition of *spyware.* It is important to include them in the discussion of *phishing* trends for the following reasons:

- **Social component:** criminals often use social engineering along with vulnerabilities in applications such as *browsers* or emails to trick users into installing malicious code on their computers.

I **Common infrastructure:** use of common tools and techniques to deliver **phishing** emails and distribute **malware**. These include the use of **botnets**, **open email relays** and compromised websites to host **phishing** and **malware** sites.

- **The big picture:** even when countermeasures are implemented to thwart one method of stealing information, criminals still have additional opportunities available to them. It is important to understand the technical capabilities of these criminals so that more effective measures to protect customer information can be developed and make tracking and punishing these criminals more effective (MILLETARY, 2005).

According to Microsoft (2008), **phishing** is a type of fraud designed to steal valuable personal data, such as credit card numbers, passwords, account details or other information.

Fraudsters can send millions of fraudulent emails that appear to come from trusted sites (such as your bank or a credit card company) and ask you to provide personal information.

These copies of websites are also classed as "**spoofed**". By unwittingly entering one of these sites, you could be sending personal information to the site's creators.

2.2.1 Spear Phishing

This term refers to a highly targeted **phishing** attack. **Spear phishers** send an email that looks authentic to all employees or members of a particular company, government body, organisation or group. **Spear phishers** can also personalise emails with information found on websites, **blogs** or social networks. They can also create fake **login** pages on social networking sites to encourage people to enter personal information on the sites they use.

While traditional **phishing** attempts aim to steal information from individuals, **spear phishing** attempts try to gain access to a company's entire system (MICROSOFT, 2006).

2.2.2 Tools Used in the Phishing Scam Technique

- *Malware: Malware* is short for *"malicious software"*. It is any *software* that has been developed to cause damage to computers, servers or networks.

Malware can do a lot of damage to your computer, such as corrupting data, slowing down your computer, using your *email* programme to spread to other computers, erasing everything from your hard drive (MICROSOFT).

- ***Bots** and **Botnets**:* A *bot*, also called a *worm bot,* is automated *software* that operates as an agent for a user or another programme. *Bots* can be used to perform *online* tasks such as checking stock prices, comparing prices or collecting and classifying documents, but they are increasingly being used for malicious purposes.

Their controllers, the *botmasters*, look for computers with open ports, through which they install their *bot* programmes. Once the computer is infected, the *bot software* orders the computer to connect to a channel that allows communication with the *botmaster* (IRC Channel - *Internet Relay Chat*).

Computers loaded with *bots* are called "zombies" by experts, since the *botmaster* can awaken them at will. When *bots* are spread to several computers, the network of affected machines, called a *botnet*, is controlled to carry out a wide range of malicious activities, such as distributing spam messages, phishing scams or recording keystrokes (HEURYS TECHNOLOGY; TREND MICRO).

Microsoft (2006) stated that *online* criminals can use certain tactics to control a large number of computers at once that can work together as a powerful "*botnet*" to carry out malicious tasks.

Botnets comprise astonishing numbers of individual "zombie" computers, which can distribute spam, spread viruses and attack other computers and servers, as well as committing other types of crime and fraud. This technique is highly valued by *online* criminals and has become a serious problem on the Internet.

- **Trojan horse:** A Trojan horse is a malicious programme that is sent as if it were a file that could lead the user to execute it. Once installed, Trojans open at least one door in the computer so that whoever sent it can have complete access to the system. Most allow the **hacker** to take full control of the PC, delete or create files, modify settings, install programmes, or even move the mouse or open the CD-ROM tray remotely (HARDWARE GUIDE).

Also known as **Trojans**, they are executable programmes that control all parts of the computer and communicate with the outside world. A **hacker** connects to the **Trojan** via an open, undocumented door in the system that allows the creator to access it (**backdoor**) and can remotely control the hacked machine (ULBRICH; DELLA VALLE, 2006).

- ***Spyware:*** Once installed, "spy" *software* gathers information about the user's browsing habits and more personal data, sending it to the owners when the user connects to the internet.

There is *spyware* used by companies that is installed alongside other programmes or even *drivers*, which basically sends some information about the user's browsing habits or the product purchased, which can be used in *marketing* campaigns, but also really malicious *spyware*, which can track the keyboard, steal passwords, etc (HARDWARE GUIDE).

- ***Spam:*** These are unsolicited emails sent en masse (sometimes to millions of users). They are usually advertising messages or commercial proposals, but there are also many cases of this type of email containing malicious and/or "infectious" attachments (MONITOR DAS FRAUDES, 2009).

2.2.3 Examples of Phishing Scams

The main examples of the *phishing* technique to be found on the Internet are the following:

- **Emails**: in this case, the attacker's email impersonates the *email* team and asks for information about the user's account, as shown in Figure 1.

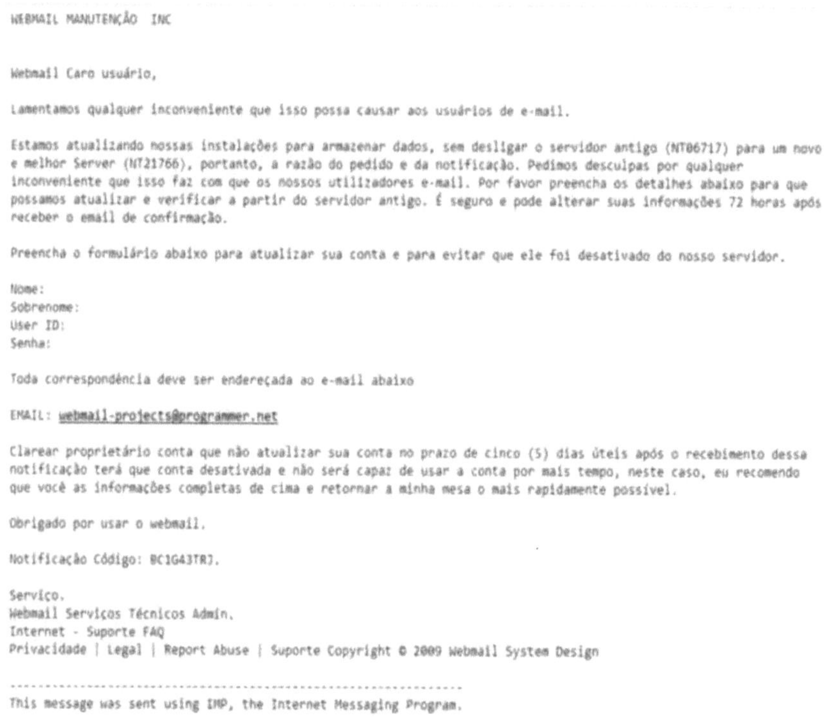

WEBMAIL MANUTENÇÃO INC

Webmail Caro usuário,

Lamentamos qualquer inconveniente que isso possa causar aos usuários de e-mail.

Estamos atualizando nossas instalações para armazenar dados, sem desligar o servidor antigo (NT06717) para um novo e melhor Server (NT21766), portanto, a razão do pedido e da notificação. Pedimos desculpas por qualquer inconveniente que isso faz com que os nossos utilizadores e-mail. Por favor preencha os detalhes abaixo para que possamos atualizar e verificar a partir do servidor antigo. É seguro e pode alterar suas informações 72 horas após receber o email de confirmação.

Preencha o formulário abaixo para atualizar sua conta e para evitar que ele foi desativado do nosso servidor.

Nome:
Sobrenome:
User ID:
Senha:

Toda correspondência deve ser endereçada ao e-mail abaixo

EMAIL: webmail-projects@programmer.net

Clarear proprietário conta que não atualizar sua conta no prazo de cinco (5) dias úteis após o recebimento dessa notificação terá que conta desativada e não será capaz de usar a conta por mais tempo, neste caso, eu recomendo que você as informações completas de cima e retornar a minha mesa o mais rapidamente possível.

Obrigado por usar o webmail.

Notificação Código: BC1G43TRJ.

Serviço.
Webmail Serviços Técnicos Admin.
Internet - Suporte FAQ
Privacidade | Legal | Report Abuse | Suporte Copyright © 2009 Webmail System Design

---

This message was sent using IMP, the Internet Messaging Program.

Figure 1 - Phishing e-mail used to steal user account information.

- **Fake websites**: Figure 2 is a perfect copy of a banking website. However, all the data entered on the site is sent directly to its creator. The correct website address would be: http://www.bradesco.com.br.

Figure 2 Fraudulent website
Source: PEIXOTO, 2006b.

More examples of the **phising** technique are given in the appendices.

2.3 Information

Basically, information has two purposes: to learn about an organisation's internal and external environments and to act in these environments (CHAUMIER, 1986).

2.3.1 The importance of information

Sêmola (2003) stated that one of the company's main values is information. It is distributed throughout all business processes, feeding them and circulating through various assets (everything that directly or indirectly handles information, including itself), environments and technologies. Information fulfils the important role of providing instruments for business management.

Information represents competitive business intelligence and is recognised as a critical asset for operational continuity and company health. The importance of information for organisations is clear, and it is at least one of the resources whose management and use are directly related to project success. Information is also considered and used in many organisations as a structuring factor and a management tool (MORESI, 2000).

2.3.2 Information Security

For Sêmola (2003), information security can be defined as an area of knowledge dedicated to protecting information against unauthorised access, undue alterations or its unavailability. He also sees it as the practice of managing the risks of events that could compromise the three main concepts of security: confidentiality, integrity and availability of information, affecting all stages of the information life cycle: handling, storage, transport and disposal, making it possible to identify and control threats and vulnerabilities.

The corporate view of information security should be compared to a chain, in which the weakest link determines its degree of resistance and protection. Invasion occurs where security fails.

2.3.3 Threats

According to Sêmola (2003), these are agents or conditions that can compromise information and its handling and processing processes by exploiting vulnerabilities, causing a loss of confidentiality, integrity and availability and, consequently, impacting an organisation's business.

They can be divided into the following groups:

- **Natural:** Threats arising from natural phenomena such as natural fires, floods, earthquakes, electromagnetic storms, tsunamis, warming, pollution, etc.

- **Involuntary:** Unconscious threats, almost always caused by ignorance. They can be caused by accidents, mistakes, lack of energy, etc.

- **Voluntary:** Purposeful threats caused by human agents such as **hackers**, intruders, spies, thieves, creators and spreaders of computer viruses, arsonists.

2.3.4 Vulnerabilities

Weakness present or associated with the processes of handling and/or processing information, which, when exploited by threats, allows a security incident to occur, negatively affecting one or more principles of information security.

Vulnerabilities alone do not cause incidents, as they are passive elements, requiring a causative agent or favourable condition, which are threats.

Examples of vulnerabilities:

- **Physical:** Substandard building facilities; poorly planned Data Processing Centre (DPC) rooms; lack of fire extinguishers, smoke detectors and other fire-fighting resources in rooms with strategic cabinets and binders, risk of explosions, leaks or fires.

- **Natural:** Computers are susceptible to natural disasters such as fires, floods, earthquakes, storms, and others such as power outages, dust accumulation, increased humidity and temperature, etc.

- ***Hardware:*** Failure of technological resources (wear, obsolescence, bad use) or errors during installation.

- ***Software:*** Errors in installation or configuration can lead to improper access, information leaks, loss of data or unavailability of the resource when needed.

- **Media:** Discs, tapes, reports and printouts can be lost or damaged. Electromagnetic radiation can affect various types of magnetic media.

- **Communication:** Unauthorised access or loss of communication.

- **Human:** Lack of training, sharing of confidential information, non-execution of security routines, errors or omissions; bomb threats, sabotage, civil disturbances, strikes, vandalism, theft, destruction of property or data, invasions or wars (SÊMOLA, 2003).

2.4 Database

According to Heuser (1998), a database is a set of data integrated with the system, the purpose of which is to serve a community of users.

Date (2000) stated that a database is a collection of persistent data used by a company's application systems.

2.4.1 Database Management System (DBMS)

The main objective of a DBMS is to provide an environment that is both convenient and efficient for retrieving and storing database information (SILBERSCHATZ et al,1999).

According to Heuser (1998), a DBMS is, in short, software that incorporates the functions of defining, retrieving and modifying data in a database.

2.4.1.1 ***MySQL***

Favan and Rall (2009) stated that MySQL is an open-source, multi-threaded, enterprise-level relational database management system that has the following characteristics: agile, compliant with international standards; has a great help system; is compatible with practically all platforms available on the market; free for non-commercial use; and has layered structures.

According to Maslakowski (2000) MySQL is a resilient database server that can work for the entire organisation. It has the advanced security measures that need to be established at this level of business. It also provides speed and flexibility that no other database in its class can match.

2.5 Personal Home Page **(PHP)**

According to Ullman (2008), PHP was originally known as **Personal Home Page** and was created in 1994 by Rasmus Lerdorf to track visitors to his **website**. Later, PHP came to stand for **Hypertext Preprocessor**, meaning that PHP handles the data before it becomes HTML.

PHP is one of the most widely used languages on the Internet.

According to Niederauer (2004), more than 10 million websites worldwide currently use PHP. The main difference with other languages is PHP's ability to interact with the **web** world, drastically changing **websites** that have static pages.

One advantage of this language is that PHP gives you the freedom to choose the most suitable operating system and web server. You can also choose procedural or object-orientated programming, or a mixture of the two (PHP DOCUMENTATION GROUP, 2003). Another advantage of this language is its connection to databases. Several databases are supported by this language, meaning that PHP has code that executes the functions of each one. These include MySQL, PostgreSQL, Sybase, Oracle, SQL Server and many others (NIEDERAUER, 2004).

According to Serrão and Marques (2000), the qualities of this tool go beyond the fact that it works in practically all known environments. It also has a zero acquisition cost, which combined with its ease of learning and use, contributes to its enormous use in programming applications for the Internet.

Another feature of this language is that when a PHP page is accessed, all the PHP code is executed on the server, and the results are sent to your browser. In this way, the browser only displays the page that has already been processed, without consuming resources from the user's computer (NIEDERAUER, 2004).

CHAPTER 3

MATERIAL AND METHODS

3.1 Materials

3.1.1 Equipment

The project used a computer - AMD *Athlon(tm)* ***64*** X2 *Dual Core* 4000+ 2.11 GHz, 2GB RAM, 160 GB Hard Disk, *Windows Seven Home Premium.*

3.1.2 Software for Development

Adobe *Dreamweaver* CS4 was also used to create the website and Navicat software was used to create the MySQL database.

3.2 Methodologies used in the study

The methodology used in the project was based on up-to-date scientific sources available on the subject of developing and analysing **Phishing Scam** technology.

It was developed by building a website with the attraction of a prize draw for a piece of technological equipment (a notebook), with participation based on registration on the site.

The site has several fields for registering various personal information, but **only the "age" and "sex" fields are linked to** the database.

The site was built in stages:

1. Creation of the database using the Navicat tool and the Mysql database described in Figures 3 to 12 respectively:

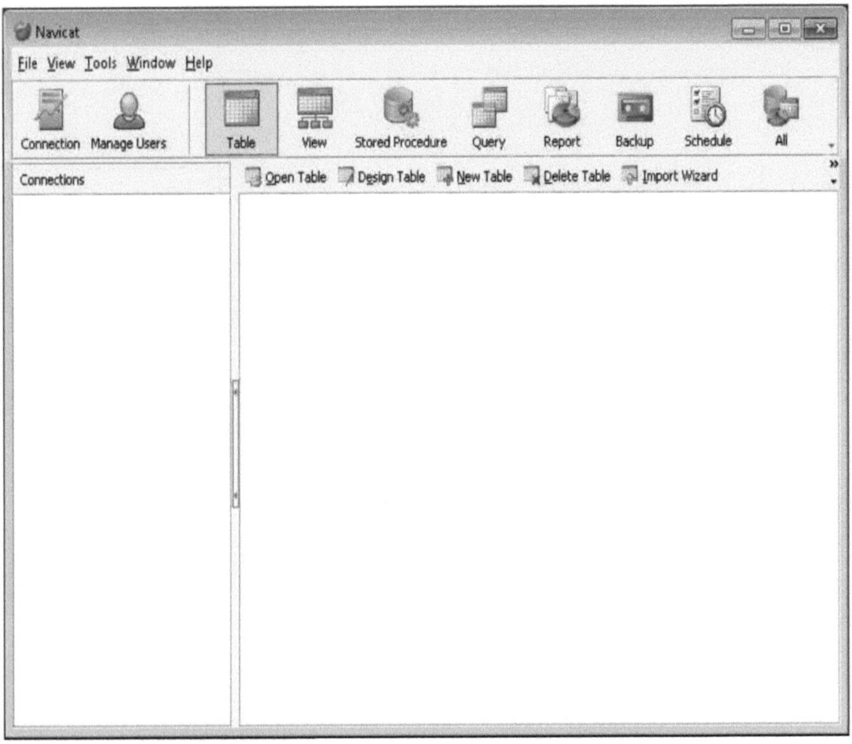

Figure 3 - Navicat **software** screen

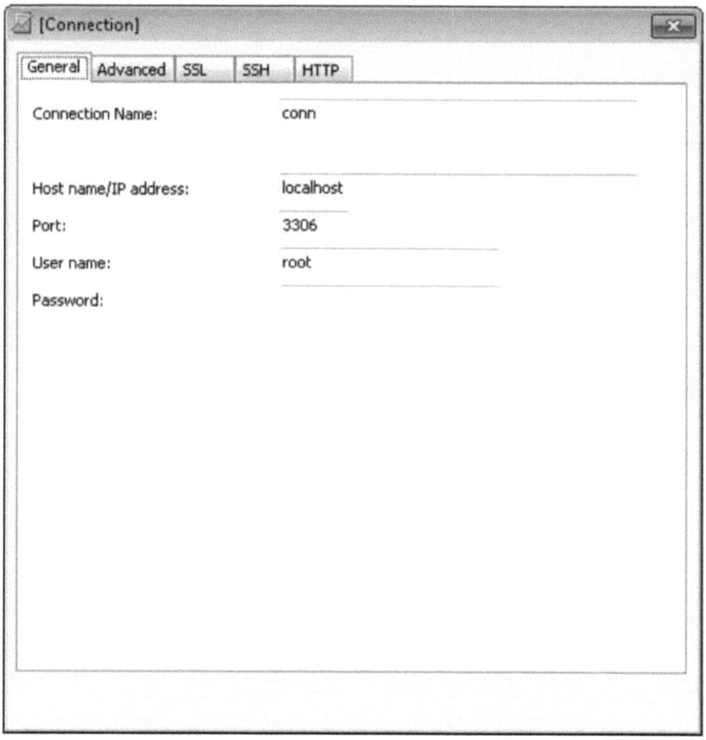

Figura 4. Creating the connection to the Navicat 1 **software**

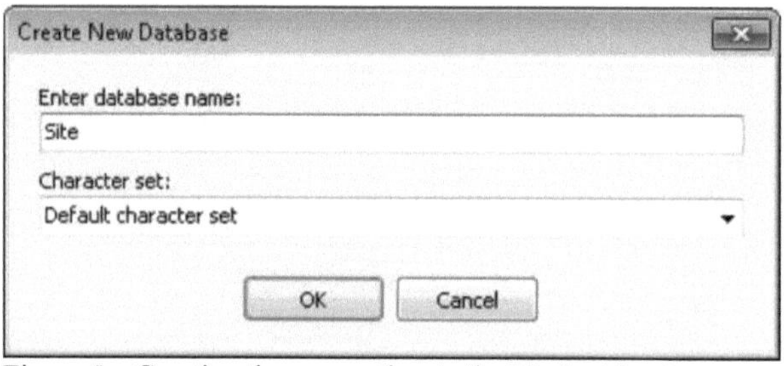

Figura 5. Creating the connection to the Navicat 2 **software**

Figure 6. Creating the tables with Navicat 1 **software**

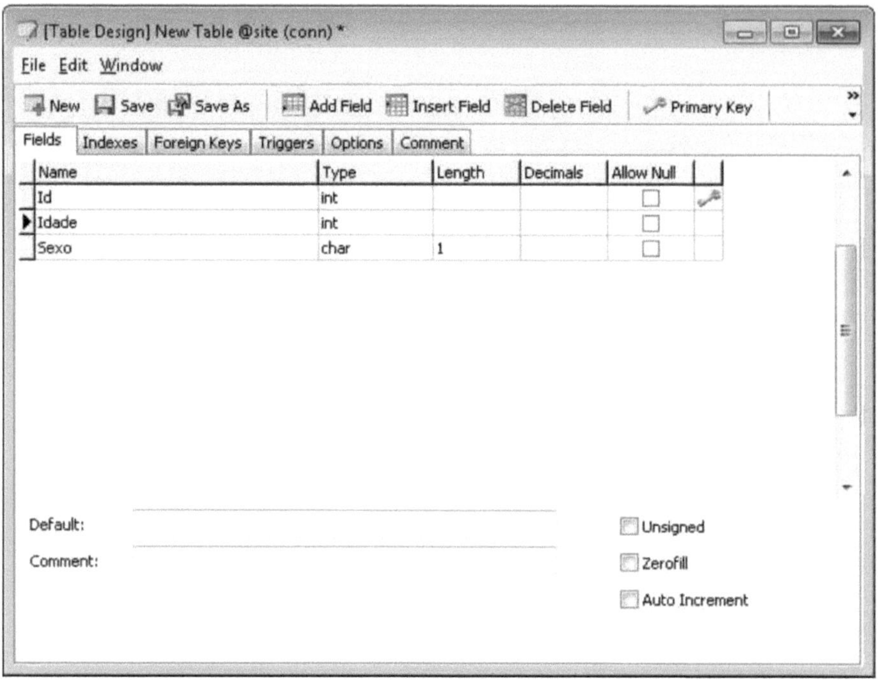

Figura 7. Creating the tables with Navicat 2 **software**

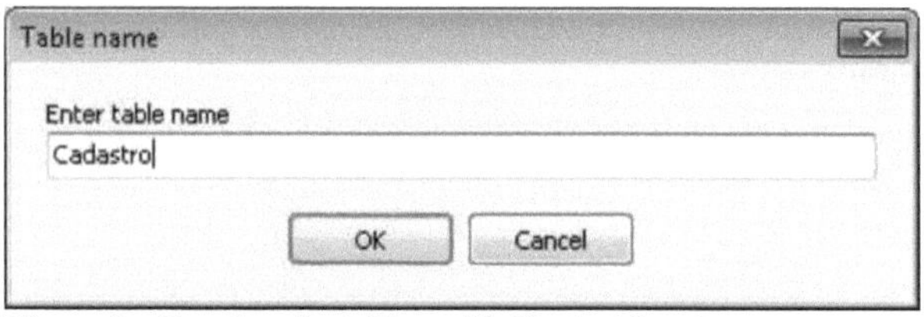

Figura 8. Creating the tables with Navicat 3 **software**

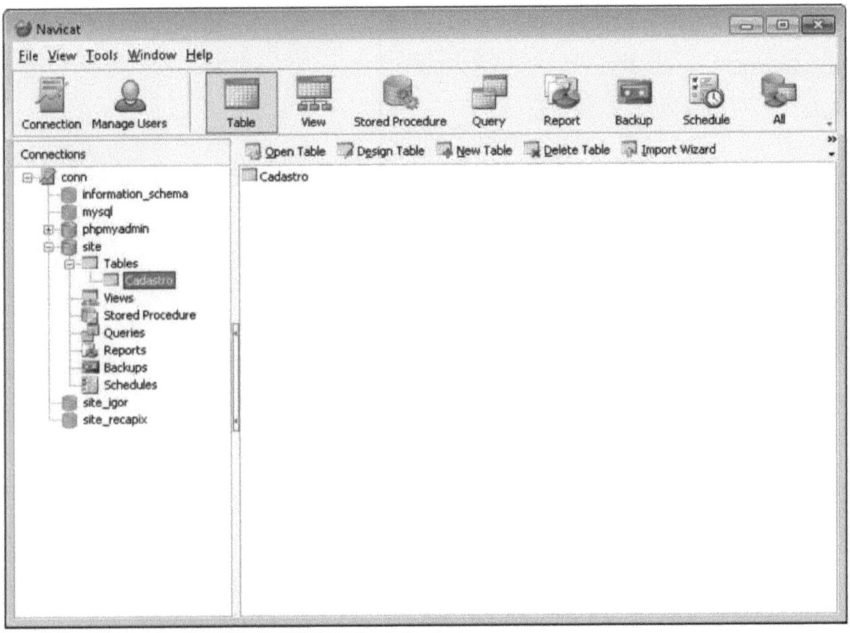

Figura 9. Creating the tables with Navicat 4 **software**

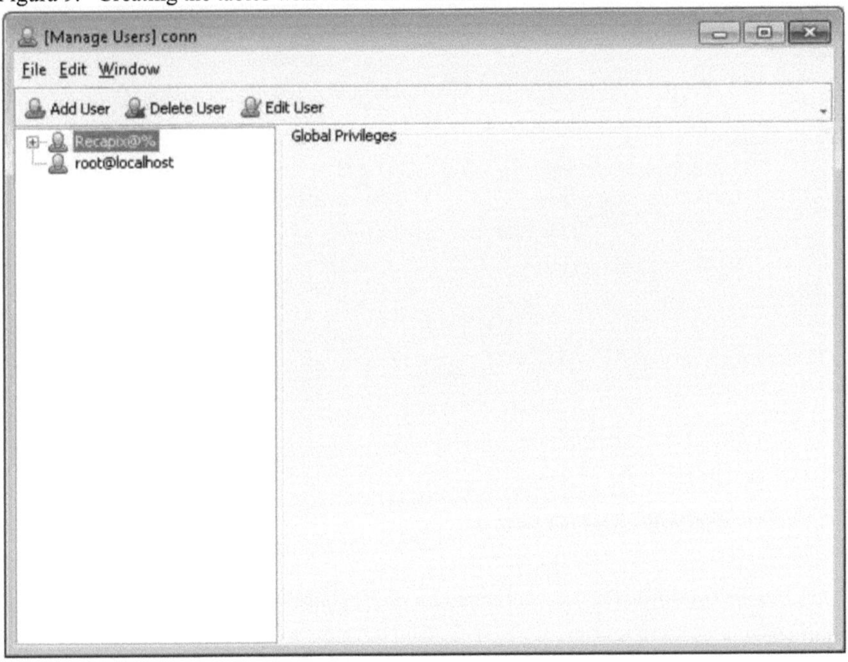

Figura 10. User creation with Navicat 1 **software**

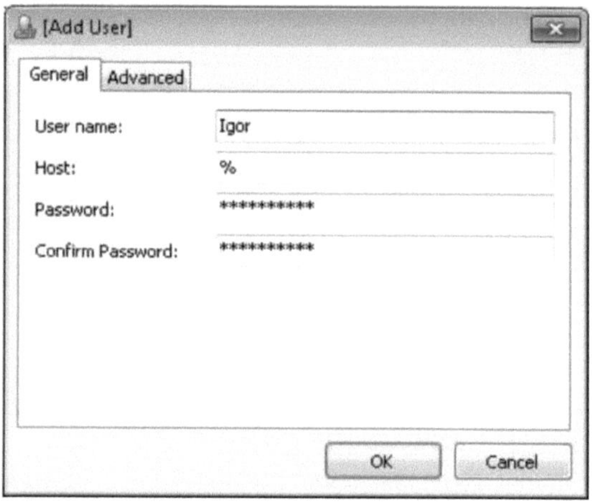

Figura 11. User creation with Navicat 2 **software**

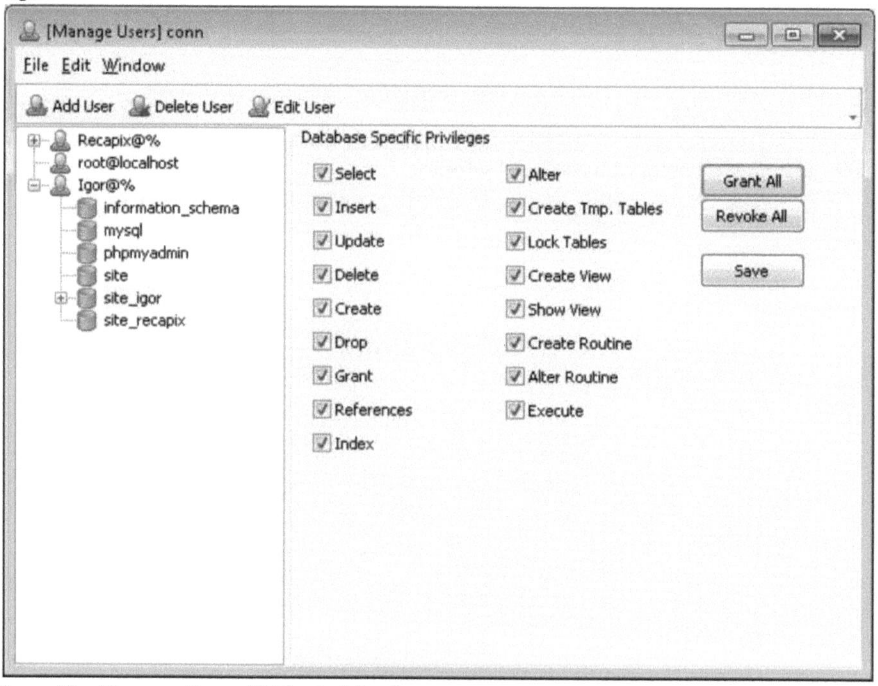

Figura 12. User creation with Navicat 3 **software**

2. Adobe **Dreamweaver** was configured for direct connections to the bank. Described in Figures 13 to 16:

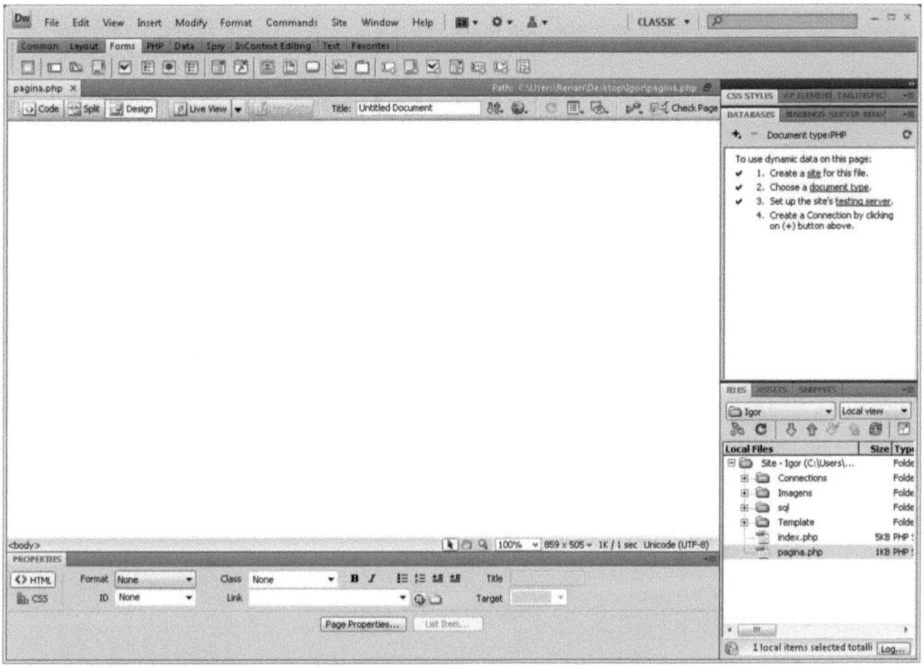

Figura 13. Adobe **Dreamweaver software** screen.

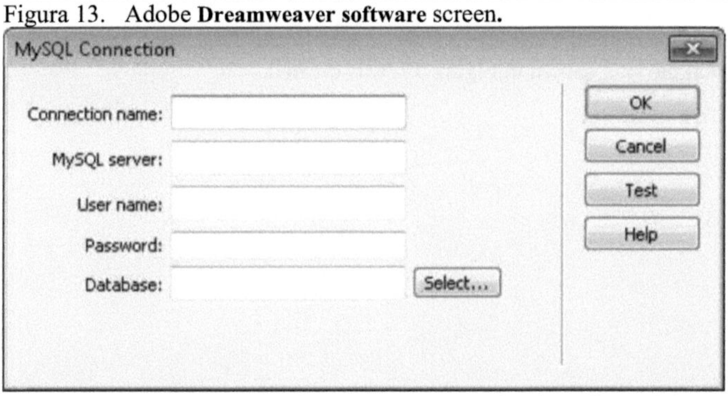

Figura 14. Creating the database connection to the site using Adobe **Dreamweaver** 1 **software**

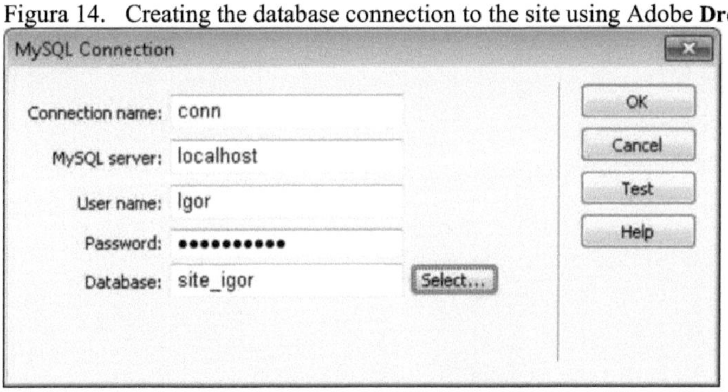

Figura 15. Creating the database connection to the site using Adobe **Dreamweaver** 2 **software**

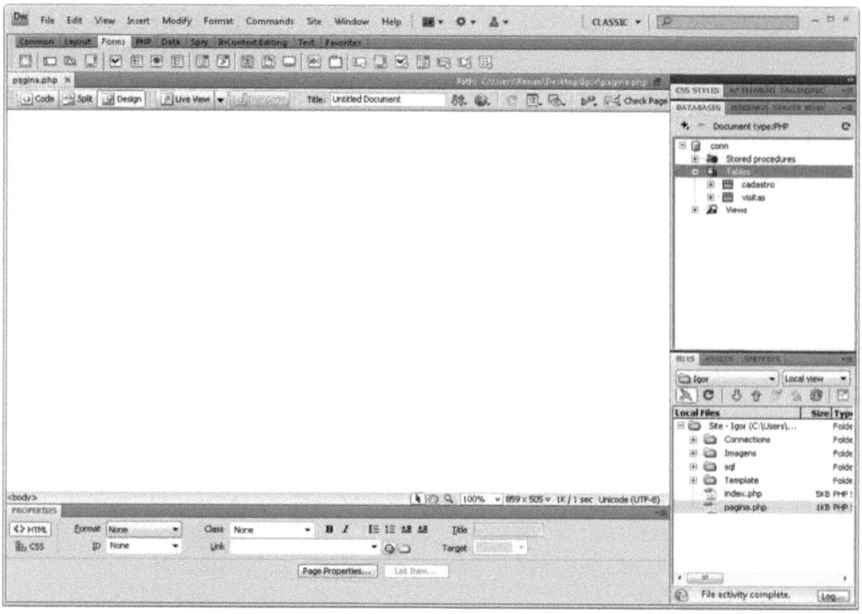

Figura 16. Creating the database connection to the site using Adobe **Dreamweaver** 3 **software**

3. The **template** used on the site, shown in Figure 17, was created:

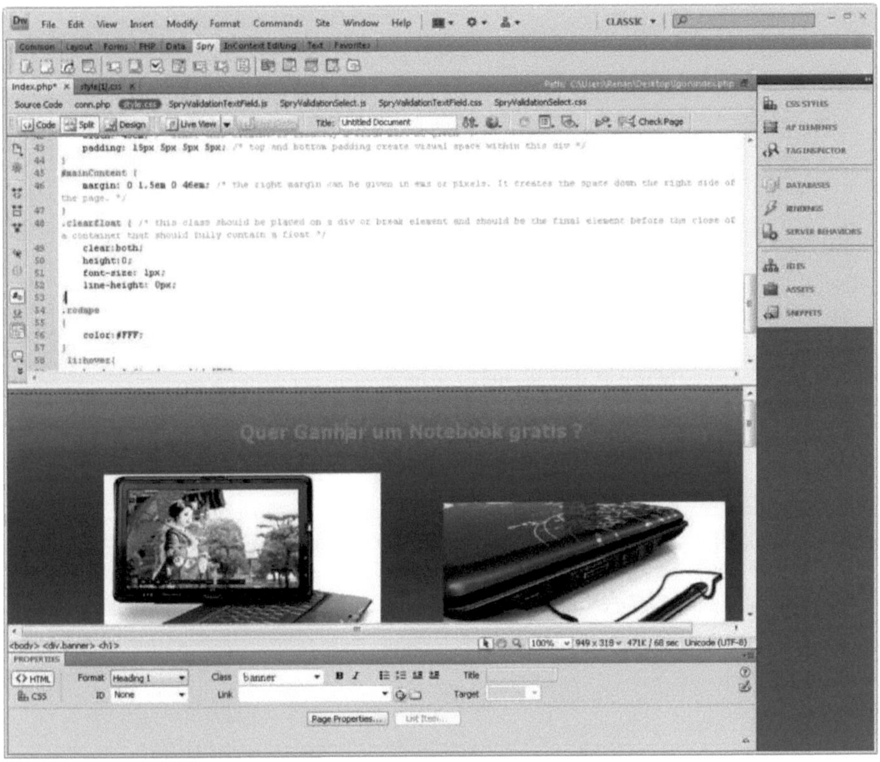

Figura 17. **Template** creation using Adobe **Dreamweaver software**

4. Then the **insert recordset** was created, the way in which the database tables relate to the website fields, shown in Figure 18, which inserts the data into the database from the form on the website.

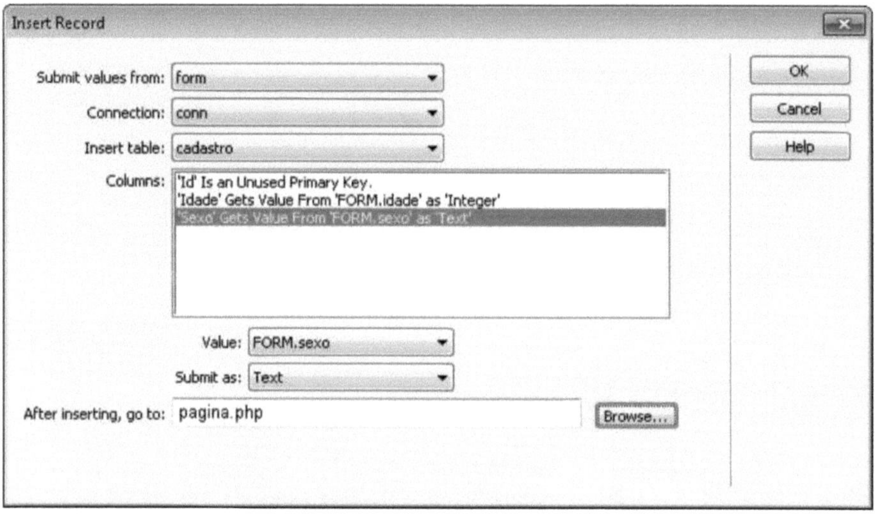

Figura 18. Creation of the **insert record set** using Adobe **Dreamweaver software.**

5. In the final stage, the site was **uploaded** to Fatec Botucatu's server, and then all the institution's computers had the site developed as their home page.

CHAPTER 4

RESULTS AND DISCUSSION

The first result was the website, shown in Figure 19:

Figura 19. Visualisation of the created site

Figura 20.

After using the site for six days, the following data was obtained, as shown in Table 1:

- **Views:** A total of 749 people viewed the site.
- **Registrations:** During the period, 465 registrations were obtained.

Table 1. Number of registrations by age.

Age	Registration		Age	Registration
17	3		36	1
18	6		37	1
19	274		38	1
20	54		39	0
21	12		40	0

22	50		41	1
23	9		42	0
24	6		43	3
25	5		44	0
26	5		45	0
27	11		46	1
28	6		47	2
29	1		48	0
30	2		49	0
31	0		50	0
32	1		51	1
33	1		52	0
34	2		53	3
35	3			

Firstly, we have a comparison of the Visualisation of the site compared to the number of registrations, as shown in Figure 20.

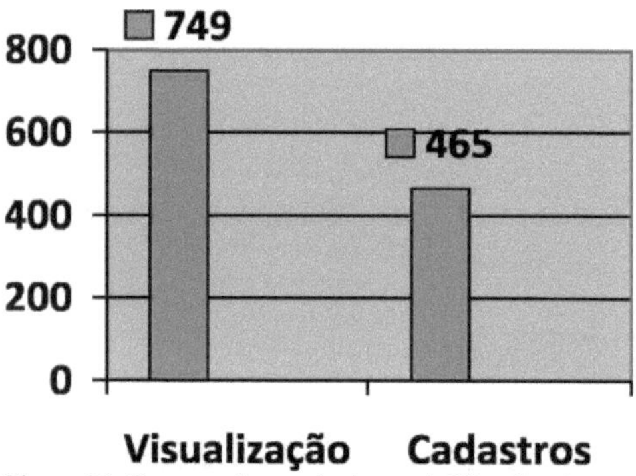

Figure 20. Comparative analysis graph Visualisation vs. Registrations

Dividing the registrations by sex reveals a large proportion of men, as shown in Figure 21.

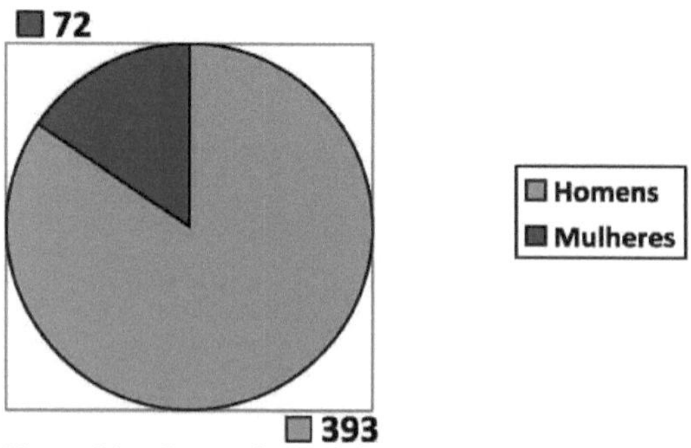

Figura 21. Comparison of the Men vs. Women register

Looking at enrolments broken down by gender, we have the following comparative data shown in Figures 22 and 23.

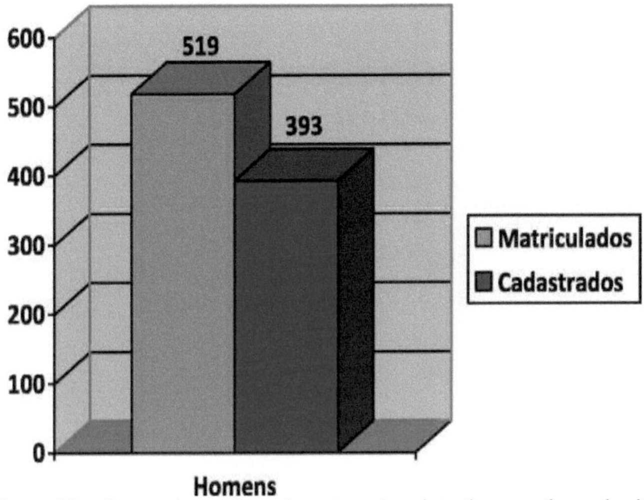

Figura 22. Comparison of enrolments and registrations on the male site.

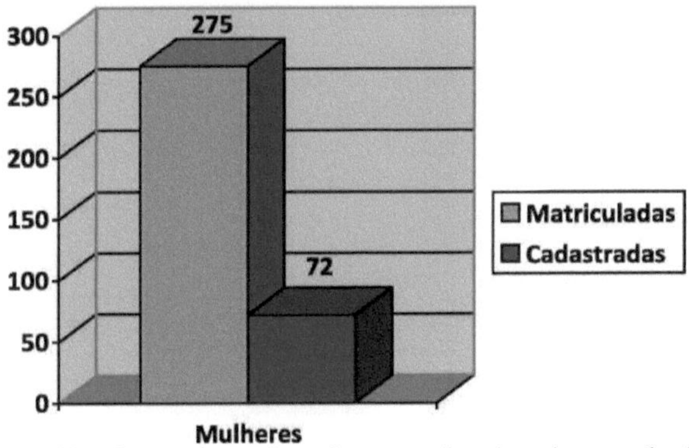

Figura 23. Comparison of enrolments and registrations on the female site.

Analysing the registrations by age group, as shown in Figure 24, we find the portion most affected by the **phishing** technique

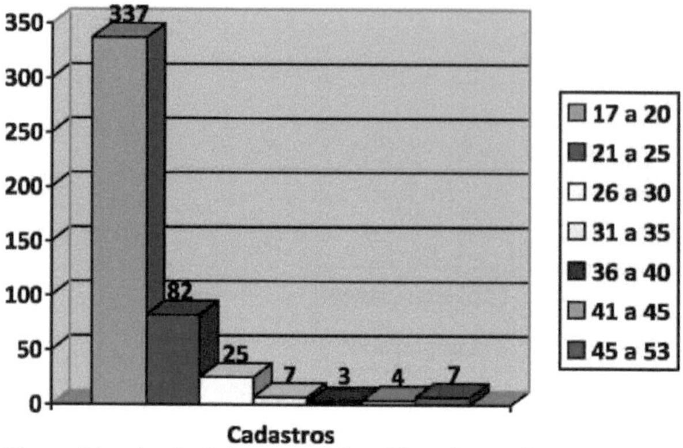

Figura 24. Analysis by age of the affected sample.

Finally, as shown in Figure 25, we have a comparative analysis of Fatec's enrolments and students.

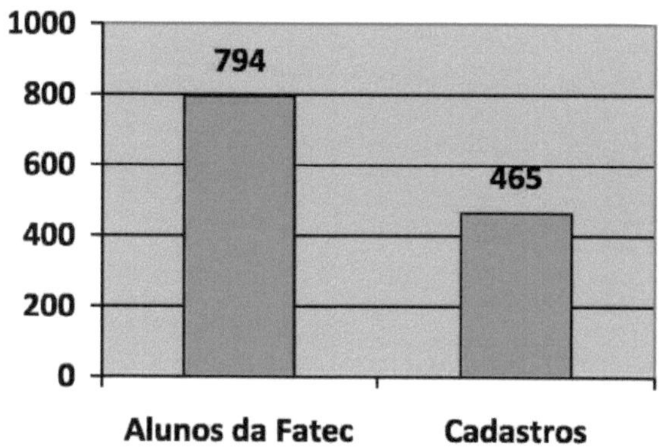

Figure 25. Comparison of Fatec Students for registered users.

CHAPTER 5

CONCLUSION

The research showed that people are easily fooled by social engineering. And the **phishing scam** technique, combined with easy gain, turns out to be a great tool for **hackers** to use.

It was also found that most people didn't even bother to check the authenticity of the site.

Nowadays, people use their computers to do market research, price quotes for products and services, access their bank accounts, do school research, and even because of a cultural problem, they end up forgetting basic security measures to protect themselves, whether it's antivirus **software** or a simple check on the authenticity of a **website** or **email**.

And of all the Fatec students who accessed the site, 58.5 per cent were caught by the technique. Of these, 85 per cent were men and only 15 per cent women. And the age group most affected was between 17 and 20 years old. This identifies the most affected group, which should be made aware of the dangers hidden behind these malicious sites.

CHAPTER 6

REFERENCES

ABNT NBR ISO/IEC 17799. **Information technology**: Code of practice for information security management. Rio de Janeiro: Brazilian Association of Technical Standards ABNT, 2005

CHAUMIER, J. Information systems**: market and technologies**. Paris: **Enterprise Moderne**, 1986.

DATE, C.J. **Introduction to Database Systems**. 7. ed. Trad. DE SOUZA, V.D. Rio de Janeiro, RJ: Editora Campus, 2000. 808 p.

DAWEL, G. **Information security in companies**: Broadening horizons beyond technology. Rio de Janeiro: Editora Ciência Moderna Ltda., 2005. 136p.

EIRAS, M. C. **Social engineering and electronic fraud**. 2004. Course conclusion paper (Latu Sensu Degree in Information Security on the Internet) - IBPI Net, Uni- Rio, Assis, 2004.- <http://www.marceloeiras.com.br/seguranca/engenharia_social.pdf>

FAVAN, J.R.; RALL,R. Analysis and development of a web system for a philanthropic institution in Botucatu. Tékhme & Logos, Botucatu, SP, v.1, n.1, p. 139-155, oct. 2009.

HARDWARE GUIDE. **Spyware Glossary**. Available at: <http://www.guiadohardware.net/termos/s.html />. Accessed on: 18 September 2009.

HARDWARE GUIDE**. Trojan Horse Glossary**. Available at: <http://www.guiadohardware.net/termos/trojan-horse>. Accessed on: 18 September 2009.

HEURYS TECNOLOGIA; TREND MICRO. **Best practices for protecting against** bots. Available at: <http://www.heurys.com.br/gxpsites/agxppdwn.aspx?2,17,337,O,P,0,501%3BP%3B1%3B61, >. Accessed on: 18 September 2009.

HEUSER,C. A. **Database Design**. 4.ed. Porto Alegre. Editora Sagra Luzzatto, 2000. 206p. Available at: <> .http://www.julianoribeiro.com.br/troca/banco_de_dados/material_der.pdf Accessed on: 07 Dec. 2009.

IGF INTELECT. **Defend yourself** - Fraud: Practical examples of phishing, May 2007. Available at:< http://www.igf.com.br/aprende/dicas/dicasResp.aspx?dica_Id=2748>. Accessed on:

23 Nov. 2009

MARCIANO, J. L.; LIMA-MARQUES, M. **The social approach to information security**. Ci. Inf. Brasília, DF, V.35, n.3, p. 89-98, Sep/Dec, 2006

MASLAKOWSKI,M. **Learn in 21 days** - mysql. Rio de Janeiro: Editora Campus, 2000. 458p.

MICROSOFT. **Know the Security Risks:** Help prevent **phishing** and **malware** with **Windows Live Messenger**. Available at: <http://www.microsoft.com/brasil/protect/yourself/learnabout/im.mspx>. Accessed on: 18 September 2009.

MICROSOFT. **Recognise** phishing **scams and fraudulent email messages**, December 2008. Available at: <http://www.microsoft.com/portugal/protect/yourself/phishing/identify.mspx>. Accessed on: 18 September 2009.

MICROSOFT. Spear Phishing: Highly targeted scams, September 2006. Available at: <http://www.microsoft.com/brasil/protect/yourself/phishing/spear.mspx>. Accessed on: 18 September 2009.

MICROSOFT. **Zombies and** Botnets: Help keep your computer under control, March 2006. Available at: <http://www.microsoft.com/brasil/athome/security/viruses/zombies_and_botnets.mspx>. Accessed on: 18 September 2009.

MILLETARY,J. ***Technical trends in phishing attacks.*** **-** US-CERT. 2005 Available at: < http://www.us-cert.gov/reading_room/phishing_trends0511.pdf>. Accessed on: 18 September 2009.

MITNICK, K. D.; SIMON, W. L. **The Art of Deception: Hacker** Attacks: Controlling the Human Factor in Information Security. 4.ed. São Paulo: Editora **Pearson Makron Books**, 2003. 284p.

FRAUD MONITOR. **Digital Security Primer:** Key Definitions, February 2009. Available at: <http://www.fraudes.org/showpage1.asp?pg=13>. Accessed on: 23 November 2009.

MORESI, E. A. D. **Outlining the value of an organisation's information system**. Ci. Inf, Brasília, DF, v.29, n.1, Jan./Apr. 2000. Available at <http://www.scielo.br/scielo.php?pid=S0100-19652000000100002&script=sci_arttext&tlng=en> Accessed on: 17 Sep. 2009.

NIEDERAUER, J. **Developing Websites with PHP**: Learn how to create dynamic and interactive websites with PHP and databases. Editora Novatec, 2004. 272p.

OLLMANN, G. The phishing guide: **Understanding and Preventing Phishing Attacks**. 2008. 40p. Available at: <http://logman.tech.officelive.com/Documents/The%20Phishing%20Guide.pdf>. Accessed on: 18 Sep. 2009.

PEIXOTO, M. C. P. P. **Social engineering and information security**: in Corporate Management. Rio de Janeiro: Editora Brasport, 2006. 132p.

PEIXOTO, M. C. P. P. **Social engineering and information security:** in corporate management. Rio de Janeiro: Editora Brasport 2006. 1 CD-ROM

PHP DOCUMENTATION GROUP. **PHP Manual**, January 2003. Available at: <http://www.daimi.au.dk/~bouvin/hyper03/php/PHP_Manual.pdf>. Accessed on: 3 Dec. 2009.

SÊMOLA, M. **Information Security Management**: An Executive View. 10.ed. Rio de Janeiro: Editora Elsevier, 2003. 156.p

SÊMOLA, M. Your rubbish could be worth millions. Aug, 2000. Available at: <http://www.semola.com.br/disco/Coluna_IDGNow_22.pdf>. Accessed on: 11 September 2009

SERRÃO,C.; MARQUES,J. **Programming with PHP**. FCA - Editora de Informática, 2000. Available at: <https://repositorio.iscte.pt/bitstream/10071/279/1/PcPHP.pdf>. Accessed on: 03 Dec. 2009.

SILBERSCHATZ, A. et al. **Database systems**. 3.ed. São Paulo-SP; Editora **Makron Books**, 1999. 1103p.

ULBRICH, H. C.; DELLA VALLE, J. **H4CK3R University**. 5.ed. São Paulo: Editora **Digerati Books**, 2006. 352p.

ULLMAN,L. PHP for the Web: **Visual QuickStart Guide**. 3.ed. Peachpit Press, 2008. 454p.

VICTÓRIA, E. M. **Gestão coorporativa**: Estudos, métodos e metodologias da engenharia social para a segurança da informação. Final course work (Technologist in Informatics: Emphasis on Business Management) - Botucatu College of Technology, Botucatu, 2007

CHAPTER 7

APPENDIX 1

Phishing techniques applied to websites

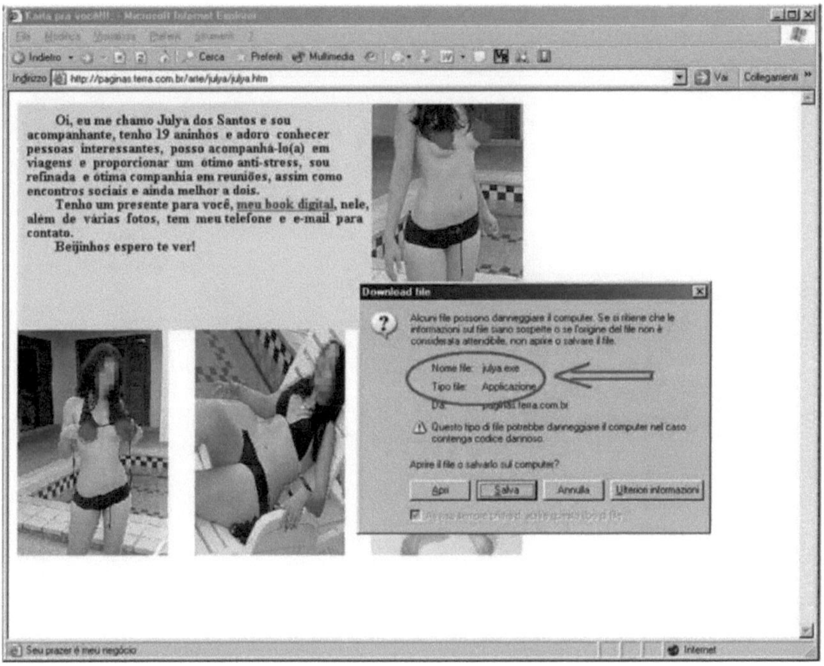

Figura 26. Website using pornography as a lure to install **malware** on the victim's computer.
Source: IGF Intelect, 2007

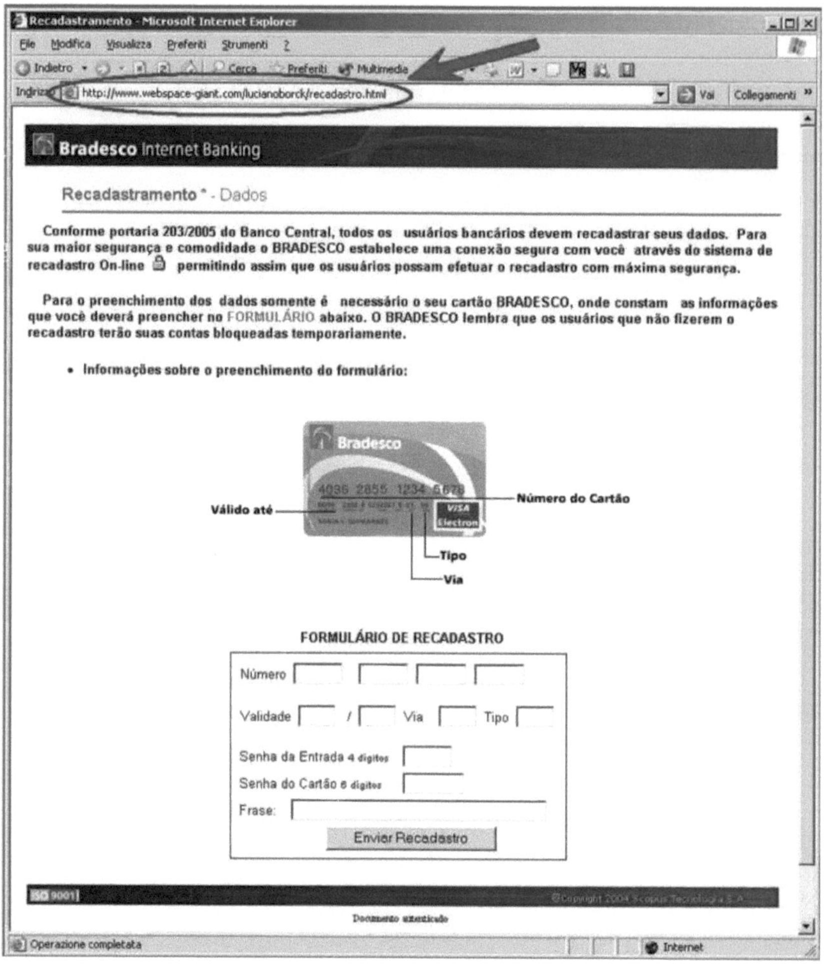

Figura 27. Fake website for a data re-registration operation to steal bank account information.
Source: IGF Intelect, 2007

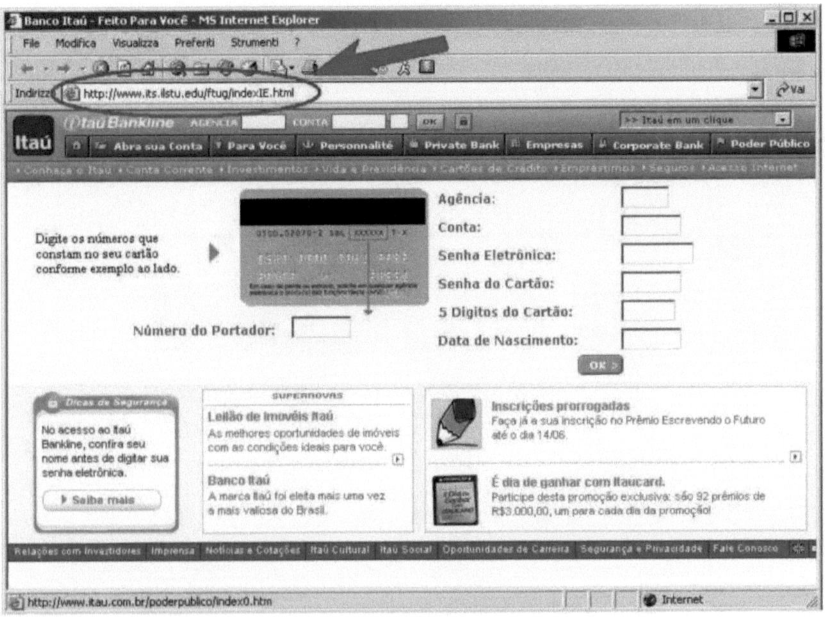

Figura 28. Fake banking website used to steal account holders' information
Source: IGF Intelect, 2007

APPENDIX 2

Phishing technique applied to **emails**

From: Banco do Brasil
To: correcao@bb.com.br
Sent: Friday, October 30, 2009 1:24 PM
Subject: BB: Componente de correcao do Cadastramento de Computadores

Componente de segurança
Atualização do Cadastramento de computadores

Componente de correção do Cadastramento de Computadores

Prezado Cliente,

Foi lançada uma nova correção para o Cadastramento de Computadores, esta corrige uma falha de nível crítico do sistema de identificação do cliente, que pode ocasionar perdas de dados e problemas no acesso.

A atualização é simples, rápida e segura, basta clicar no link abaixo e em seguida clicar em salvar e logo após executar, aguarde alguns segundos e siga as instruções.

Erro! O nome de arquivo não foi especificado.http://bancodobrasil.com.br/cadastrar/

Caso o link não funcione, clique aqui para baixar.

Atenção: Todos os usuários devem se cadastrar e atualizar o Cadastramento de Computadores. Caso a correção não seja realizada, seu computador será bloqueado e o desbloqueio poderá ser realizado somente nas agências.

Em caso de dúvidas, ligue para Central de Atendimento BB,
Capitais e Regiões Metropolitanas: 4004 0001
Demais localidades: 0800 729 0001

© Banco do Brasil

Figura 29. **E-mail** requesting registration so that the user can use **online** banking services

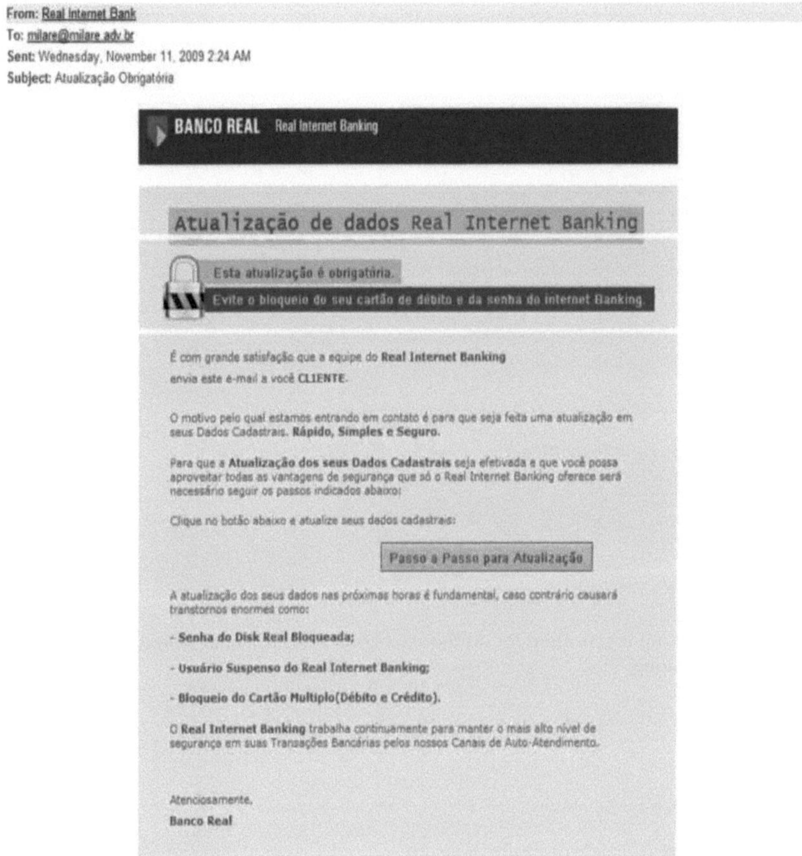

From: Real Internet Bank
To: milare@milare.adv.br
Sent: Wednesday, November 11, 2009 2:24 AM
Subject: Atualização Obrigatória

BANCO REAL Real Internet Banking

Atualização de dados Real Internet Banking

Esta atualização é obrigatória.

Evite o bloqueio do seu cartão de débito e da senha do internet Banking.

É com grande satisfação que a equipe do **Real Internet Banking** envia este e-mail a você **CLIENTE**.

O motivo pelo qual estamos entrando em contato é para que seja feita uma atualização em seus Dados Cadastrais. **Rápido, Simples e Seguro.**

Para que a **Atualização dos seus Dados Cadastrais** seja efetivada e que você possa aproveitar todas as vantagens de segurança que só o Real Internet Banking oferece será necessário seguir os passos indicados abaixo:

Clique no botão abaixo e atualize seus dados cadastrais:

Passo a Passo para Atualização

A atualização dos seus dados nas próximas horas é fundamental, caso contrário causará transtornos enormes como:

- Senha do Disk Real Bloqueada;

- Usuário Suspenso do Real Internet Banking;

- Bloqueio do Cartão Multiplo(Débito e Crédito).

O **Real Internet Banking** trabalha continuamente para manter o mais alto nível de segurança em suas Transações Bancárias pelos nossos Canais de Auto-Atendimento.

Atenciosamente,

Banco Real

Figura 30. **E-mail** requesting updated data to avoid blocking of card and **internet banking** password.

From: Bradesco S/A
To:
Sent: Saturday, November 07, 2009 4:19 AM
Subject: DDA Bradesco

DDA Bradesco

Prezado Cliente,

Comunicamos que desde o dia 19 de outubro de 2009 será obrigatório o cadastramento no DDA Bradesco para o acesso ao Internet Banking Bradesco, caso não seja feito o cadastramento seu acesso ao Internet Banking Bradesco será bloqueado.

Com o Débito Direto Autorizado Bradesco você não precisa mais se preocupar com boletos de papel, basta se cadastrar para concentrar tudo aqui no Bradesco e pagar* eletronicamente onde você estiver, de uma maneira muito mais fácil e cômoda.

Cadastre-se agora no DDA Bradesco.

Banco Bradesco-S/A.

Atenção: O cadastramento do DDA Bradesco só serão efetuadas após a confirmação dos dados (próximo acesso).

Bradesco

Todos os direitos reservados. Banco Bradesco S/A

Figura 31. **E-mail** requesting registration for Authorised Direct Debit, under penalty of being blocked from **internet banking.**

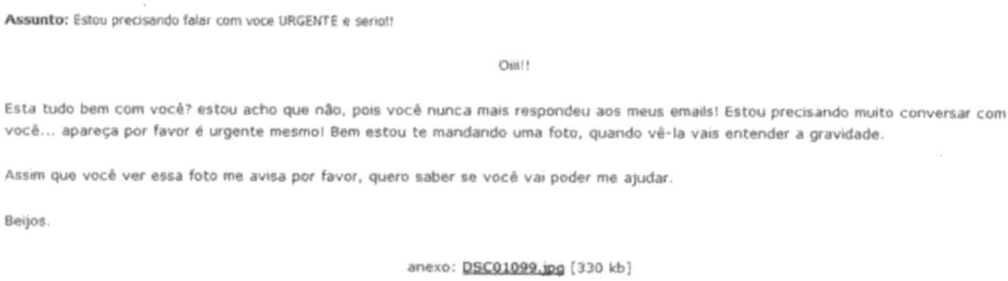

Assunto: Estou precisando falar com voce URGENTE e serio!!

Oiii!!

Esta tudo bem com você? estou acho que não, pois você nunca mais respondeu aos meus emails! Estou precisando muito conversar com você... apareça por favor é urgente mesmo! Bem estou te mandando uma foto, quando vê-la vais entender a gravidade.

Assim que você ver essa foto me avisa por favor, quero saber se você vai poder me ajudar.

Beijos.

anexo: DSC01099.jpg [330 kb]

Figura 32. **E-mail** using social engineering to get the user to download the fake attachment.

De: PROGRAMMER WEBMAIL HELPDESK UNIDADE [mailto:webmaster@programmer.br]
Enviada em: sexta-feira, 23 de outubro de 2009 12:52
Para: undisclosed-recipients:
Assunto: IMEDIATA conta de manutenção UPDATE, POR FAVOR TRATAR AS UGent ...

Caro usuário,

Esta é a nossa notificatio final para você em nosso atualização da conta. A unidade do programa do seu cliente de webmail desculpas por qualquer inconveniente que isso possa causar aos nossos usuários e-mail/webmail.

Estamos atualizando nossas instalações de armazenamento de dados, sem desligar o servidor antigo (NT06717ZZ) para um novo e melhor Server (NT21766AZ), o que a razão do pedido e da notificação. Pedimos desculpas por

qualquer inconveniente que isso fará com que o nosso e-mail respeitado e usuários de webmail. Por favor preencha os dados abaixo para que possamos atualizar e verificar a partir do servidor antigo (NT06717ZZ). É seguro e pode alterar suas informações de 72 horas após receber o email de confirmação.

Preencha os dados abaixo para atualizar.

Nome completo:
Login D:
Senha:
Data de Nascimento:

Todas as correspondências devem ser endereçadas para o endereço de e-mail abaixo
EMAIL: responds@programmer.net

Atenção! Conta do proprietário que não atualiza suas contas dentro do prazo,

após o recebimento dessa notificação perderá o acesso ao nosso serviço de webmail.

Notificação Código: BC1G43TRJ: conta de manutenção ...

Webmail Programmer Team

Em seu serviço.
Serviços Admin. Internet Suporte Técnico - FAQ
Privacidade | Legal | Report Abuse | Suporte © Copyright 2009

Figura 33. **E-mail** posing as a company **Helpdesk** to steal user account information.

Prezado Cliente,

O Bradesco trabalha continuamente para manter o mais alto nível de segurança em suas transações contábeis. Por isso, disponibilizamos o Componente de Segurança para instalação em seu computador.

Ao utilizar o Componente de Segurança Bradesco, o Cliente agrega mais segurança às transações efetuadas por meio do Bradesco Internet Banking, pois esse dispositivo somente poderá ser acionado pelo cliente.

1. Descrição. O Componente de Segurança é um software acoplado ao seu navegador para ampliar suas funções de segurança, na realização de transações contábeis no Canal **Bradesco Internet Banking**.

2. Finalidade. O Componente de Segurança tem por finalidade atuar na detecção/inibição de softwares maliciosos, a exemplo do vírus cavalo-de-tróia, usados para capturar as informações inseridas por meio do teclado do computador convencional e virtual, durante o acesso ao Bradesco Internet Banking e monitoramento/armazenamento de informações do hardware (dados criptografados não contendo informações pessoais) do cliente utilizado para identificação da origem do acesso.

3. Funcionamento. Com a conclusão da instalação, o Componente de Segurança terá sua ativação inicializada quando da utilização do produto Bradesco Internet Banking, não sendo válido para outros sites. O Componente não elimina as eventuais vulnerabilidades que possam existir nos computadores dos usuários do produto.

4. Instalação/ Atualização. Quando o sistema identificar que o Componente de Segurança não está instalado em seu computador, será enviado um e-mail com um link para download do software.
As atualizações do Componente de Segurança, serão efetuadas após a conclusão da instalação (próximo acesso) caso haja necessidade e, serão executadas automaticamente sem que haja interferência na navegação.

Para efetuar a instalação, clique em **Instale já**.

Obs: As contas dos Titulares (1º/2º/3º) estarão automaticamente associadas.

Figura 34. **E-mail** impersonating **Internet Banking by** installing **malware**.

From: marina@unip.br
To: candeias@ibb.unesp.br
Sent: Thursday, September 24, 2009 5:17 PM
Subject: de coração, uma pequena recordação do motel

Anexo: na cama.jpg (386,7 KB) na banheira.jpg (227,8 KB) de quatro.jpg (98,8 KB)

Nossa foi demais ter passado o dia com você no motel, que dia podemos ir denovo ?

Deleta essas fotos depois que ver elas, ou entao grave em cd.. mas nao deixe no seu e-mail, pode ser perigoso.

Me liga mais tarde pq preciso falar com você ! Beijos.

Figura 35. **E-mail** using social engineering and fake attachments to install **malware**.

From: Julyana90
To: ylmores@ibb.unesp.br
Sent: Thursday, September 17, 2009 10:55 PM
Subject: No jeitinho.... ;)

ATENÇÃO: Se você não conseguir visualizar o conteúdo desta mensagem, selecione a opção: **"Mostrar conteúdo"** para visualizar corretamente esta mensagem.

Oi, eu falei que ia fazer um álbum especial pra vc..
estão ai todas... tem cada uma, não espalha tá !!!!!
separei essa ai so pra vc, o resto está no book.
depois manda um email dizendo o que achou tá bebê!

Beijosss... =*

Book da Julyana90

Figura 36. **E-mail** using social engineering and a **link**, leading to the installation of **malware**.

MIX
Papier aus verantwortungsvollen Quellen
Paper from responsible sources
FSC® C105338

Printed by Books on Demand GmbH, Norderstedt / Germany